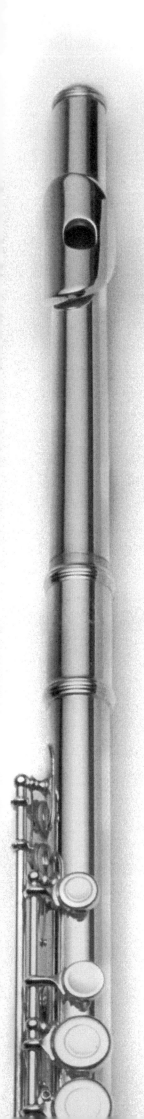

Trevor Wye
PRACTICE BOOK
for the Flute
Book 3
Articulation

Contents

PREFACE 3

ARTICULATION–General 5

  a) Slurs 5

  b) Single Tonguing 10

  c) Double Tonguing 16

  d) Triple Tonguing 25

  e) The E♭ problem 28

NERVES 31

EXAMPLES 32

Novello

Published by
Novello Publishing Limited

Exclusive Distributors:
Hal Leonard
7777 West Bluemound Road
Milwaukee, WI 53213
Email: info@halleonard.com

Hal Leonard Europe Limited
42 Wigmore Street
Marylebone, London, W1U 2RY
Email: info@halleonardeurope.com

Hal Leonard Australia Pty. Ltd.
4 Lentara Court
Cheltenham, Victoria, 3192 Australia
Email: info@halleonard.com.au

Order No. NOV164142
ISBN 978-1-78305-421-3

Edited by Toby Knowles.
Music engraved by Paul Ewers Music Design.

Printed in the EU.

The Practice Book series is about effective practice: how to extract the most from it, how to be more skilled at it and how to isolate and overcome the problems and difficulties encountered in performing. It was written to help you achieve good results in the shortest time. If the advice is followed and the exercises practised properly, they will shorten the time taken to achieve success in the basics of flute playing and music making.

Practising

Practise because you want to. If you don't want to – don't. It is almost useless spending your practice time practising, but wishing that you weren't. Having decided to practise seriously, make it difficult. Examine all aspects of your tone, intonation and technique for flaws and practise to remove them. You will then make rapid progress. Practise what you can't play, or practise a technique you are not familiar with. Try not to indulge in too much self-flattery by playing through pieces or exercises you can already play well.

Many of these exercises are strenuous so be sure your posture and hand positions are correct. Consult a good teacher or if you are in doubt, refer to *Practice Book 6 – Advanced Practice* (NOV164175) or look at *Efficient Practice* (Trevor Wye; Falls House Press), or *Proper Flute Playing* (NOV120651), the companion book to the *Practice Book* series, which contains a guide on how best to schedule these exercises.

How to make the best use of your practice time

Most of us have a limit on how much time we have to practise. Let's assume that the four subjects below are the priority. Each should take up about one quarter of your total technical practice time, though this can be varied according to needs:

Tone • Expression and Intonation • Technique • Scales and Arpeggios

Articulation needs extra time, although if your articulation is good, you can incorporate this into scales and technique sessions by varying the articulation patterns as shown in *Practice Book 2 – Technique* (NOV164131) and *Practice Book 5 – Breathing & Scales* (NOV164164). This book suggests ways to achieve clear and rapid tonguing effectively. Of course you will have other subjects to work on too, but this is a practical scheme which will help most people. Technique (finger independence) is not quite the same as scales and arpeggios, which are the building blocks of musical composition. Scales and arpeggios are set out in *Practice Book 5* and in *The Complete Daily Exercises* (NOV120850). Technique and finger independence exercises can be found in *Practice Book 2* and also in *Practice Book 6 – Advanced Practice*.

GUARANTEE

Possession of this book is no guarantee that you will improve on the flute; there is no magic in the printed paper. But, if you have the desire to play well and if you put in some diligent practice, you cannot fail to improve. It is simply a question of *time*, *patience* and *intelligent* work. The book is designed to avoid unnecessary practice. It is concentrated stuff. Provided that you follow the instructions carefully, you should make more than twice the improvement in half the time!

That is the guarantee.

This is one of a series of six books for players of all ages who have been learning the flute from about a year upwards and including those at college or university. The material has been spread out over the six books and should be selected and practised as needed. The speed of the exercises should be chosen to accommodate the skill and age of the player. Some exercises are more difficult than others. Simply use those that are the most useful.

The other books in this series are:

PRACTICE BOOK for the Flute

Book 1   Tone
Book 2   Technique
Book 4   Intonation & Vibrato
Book 5   Breathing & Scales
Book 6   Advanced Practice

These books were revised and updated in 2013.
© Trevor Wye

A Plan For Using This Book

It is best to read the opening section on **ARTICULATION** and **THE USE OF THE SLUR** first, and to try it out, though this can be done at a later time if preferred.

ARTICULATION SINGLE TONGUING and **THE USE OF THE ABDOMINAL MUSCLES**:

Articulation is best practised in small but frequent sessions during the practice of other exercises. Then, bit by bit, daily exercises, scales, and other material can be altered with tongued and slurred notes to accommodate the new skill. It is better in the long term to learn double tonguing only when a rapid speed in single tonguing has been achieved.

ARTICULATION CRACKING NOTES and the **E♭ EXERCISES** can be looked at any time when necessary.

ARTICULATION

Articulation is the speech of music. No matter how powerful or compelling your musical ideas, they will not be communicated to the listener unless your articulation is clear. In the English language, when we talk about someone being articulate, we mean they can express themselves. It is the same in music, though flautists mean two things by the word articulation: the use of slurs and dots and the use of the tongue. Both of these definitions will be discussed in this book.

There will be additional exercises to train your tongue to be able to respond to the demands of both the flute solo and of orchestral literature. Sometimes, a particular articulation has to be 'switched on' with immediate effect and in this book you will train your tongue to do this, and to respond to unusual articulations.

Your teacher will advise you on the best way to start, but if you are working alone, some guidance has been suggested for each section.

The Use of the Slur

Throughout musical history, slurs were most often used to add variety to a phrase, and to put emphasis on a note. Two notes slurred together add emphasis to the first, and diminish the second in importance. Very broadly, a slur is a *diminuendo*; that is the effect of a slur on two or more notes. The instruments of the 17th and 18th centuries also influenced how a slur was used, for example, the interval of a fifth or a bigger interval was not usually slurred when played on the flute. This was because the instruments did not lend themselves to slurring large intervals easily, as our modern flute does so well.

The slur is also useful in grouping together patterns of notes so as to make a passage flow better or to make the language clearer. For example, the great 18th Century teacher, J.J. Quantz, shows that melodic patterns might be grouped together as in the first example shown here. In the second example, sharp rhythmic contrast is slurred which would otherwise sound rough; and in the third example, rhythmic patterns are grouped together by slurs:

In other periods and in other countries, composers wrote slurs for different reasons such as for variety or sometimes – perhaps in the case of some pianists – because they didn't clearly understand how powerful the slur can be on a wind instrument.

If you keep in mind that, whatever other reasons there are for slurring notes together, the result must make the musical idea clear to your audience.
A slur over two notes raises the importance of the first and diminishes the importance of the second.
A slur is a diminuendo – except sometimes!
There are many examples of how this simple rule can be broken but for the moment, it is better to learn the rule, and then learn how to break it.

The following pattern can be played as written. However, you might decide to add slurs to it.

The performer – you – will have to decide if some notes are more important than others in that phrase. Let us assume that the 1st, 3rd 5th and 7th notes are more important:

Of course you *could* just accent them, though this is a cruder way of showing emphasis. It is simpler and more effective to slur them like this:

If you consider these notes to be more important:

Then you would place the slurs like this:

No matter how these notes above are played, the listener hears some notes as more important than others. Here are other examples using the same notes. In each case, the notes on the left are the ones the composer wants his listener to be more aware of; the passage on the right is how the slurs should be placed go get that effect:

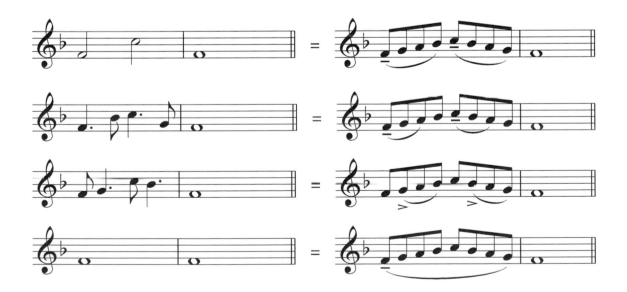

The notes on the left are sometimes referred to as the 'skeleton' or the 'bones' of the phrase.

Let's look at a real example, that of C.P.E. Bach's Sonata in E♭, 1st Movement (though often attributed to J.S. Bach). In example A, the player can simply tongue all the notes making them uniformly important. Alternatively, the player may prefer to emphasise the 1st, 5th and 7th notes in each bar, in which case the slurs should be added to reflect this idea. In Example B, bar 2, the usual interpretation might be to slur in pairs. Using too many slurs can sound bumpy. Of course, this also depends on how they are played.

SONATA NO. 2 IN E♭

C. P. E. BACH

In the Mozart, Example C, the orchestral parts may suggest slurring the first two notes of the first three groups of four, leaving the scale without a slur halfway up. Whole scales in Mozart, apart from the first two notes of the scale, are often best left tongued. In example D, there are several ways to play this, though a common solution would be to slur the first two notes of each bar, then also slurring the last two pairs in the first two bars, again leaving the scale intact after the first two slurred notes. Find your own solutions to the D Major Concerto – and if possible, consult a relevant piano accompaniment or orchestral score to help you decide what to do.

CONCERTO IN D

MOZART

CONCERTO IN G

MOZART

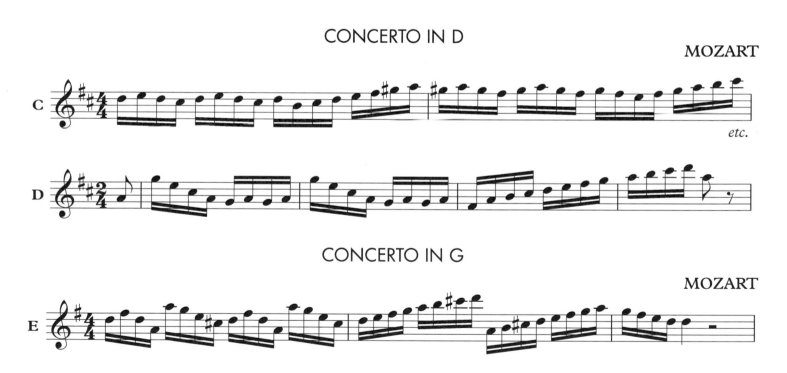

When you have decided how to slur, mark them in the part, then play them. Then justify what you have written by observing the rule that a 'slur is a *diminuendo*'.

Therefore when you play:

Phrase it like this:

7

Similarly, this passage:

Is performed like this:

Of course, if you believe that all of the notes are of equal importance, you should tongue all of them, or slur all of them; it really depends on the piece, the acoustics of the place of performance and the relevant accompaniment. String instruments can sustain notes: a piano less so, and a harpsichord or guitar less still. A performance in a church or other hall with a considerable echo will need a clear articulation and shorter notes so as to be heard at the back of the hall. The style of the piece should also be taken into consideration.

It must be apparent that this rule of the slur is just a basis on which to start editing the music. Once a decision has been made on where to place slurs, they should be performed so that the first note of the slur is given importance by tonguing it and the subsequent notes played less loudly.

Here are more examples from the flute repertoire:

SONATA IN G MINOR

C.P.E. BACH
(attrib. J. S. BACH)

In this next passage:

If you feel that the skeleton or underlying melody is:

Then place the slurs and perform it like this:

But, on the other hand, if you think Bach meant this:

Then slur like this:

etc.

Then again, if you think the composer meant:

etc.

Then play it like this:

etc.

Remember that when performing a slur, it places emphasis on the first note and diminishes the remainder. Perform them like that because it makes little sense to play them another way. If you don't agree with the slurs, change them.

Practise the six scales below, placing the emphasis where shown. Generally, avoid shortening the second note of pairs of slurred notes.

Remember what you have learned and apply these rules to all exercises which contain slurs.

ARTICULATION Single Tonguing

The study of articulation is vital to achieve a good level of performing skill on the flute and single tonguing is the most important articulation skill of all. We do use 'double tonguing' and 'triple tonguing' later, though it is wisest to imagine that these skills, for the present, do not exist. The reason is that a very fast single tongue will help to acquire a fast speed of both double and triple tonguing.

Other woodwind players rarely use double and triple tonguing for technical reasons, yet they manage to play difficult articulated passages with speed. We must acquire a fast, reliable and above all, clear single tonguing. It is a short cut to fluency and clarity in double and triple tonguing.

A good tone is essential to obtaining clear articulation. **Think of an articulation exercise as a tone exercise, but broken up**.

The Use of the Abdominal Muscles

Single notes are not made by the tongue but by the breath. The tongue's job is to make a clear start to the note. Notes are 'made' by the breath, and at slow speeds are made by starting and stopping the breath, the tongue merely cleaning up the start of the note. Notes are not stopped by the tongue but by the breath, though this does change when playing very fast.

To get 'bounce' and a lively character into single tonguing we use the abdominal muscles to start and stop the notes. It is the same muscle used in laughing or coughing. It must be trained to start the air moving into the flute speedily and to stop it quickly too, and this is achieved by practice in three ways: *short, fast* and later, *loud*. Practise the exercise below without using the tongue at all. Use only the abdominal muscles to start and stop each note. Begin by playing each note softly and as short as possible. After a time, try playing faster ensuring a clear silence between the notes. *Staccatissimo* is what to aim for. Some may find this difficult, but it is well worth practising for a few weeks if necessary.

As well as laying the groundwork for clear single tonguing, this exercise also strengthens the abdominal muscles so that later it will help in playing smoother octaves and in playing the upper limits of the flute's compass; it also facilitates the development of a fine vibrato as well as a vital role of supporting the tone. It's an important muscle.

Don't begin on the next section until you have made good progress with these exercises. First try *short*, then *louder*, and finally *faster*.

It is a much better exercise if you play in more keys; the full exercise of 24 keys can be found in *The Complete Daily Exercises* (Novello).

10

It is not easy to get clarity, speed and a clear tone in the first few notes of the second octave (E, F & F♯). Take care not to 'split' or crack the fourth note, F, in exercise A. When approaching this note, the air supply – now controlled by the abdominal muscles – has to be at the exactly the right speed to play the F clearly. Work at this.

Using the Tongue

In all research into articulation, it is clear that tonguing forward against the teeth – rather than at the roof of the mouth – makes for a clearer and more precise articulation.* The tip of the tongue should be touching the lower part of the front teeth. The principle behind this is that the tongue, which acts as a valve, can stop and start the note with precision and speed when it is closest to the place where the tone is produced – the lips.** This action may not at first feel entirely comfortable for some, especially for those who find difficulty in pointing the tongue, but with practice, it will get easier.

Practise the same exercise as before, adding the tongue, but still using the abdominal muscles to control the air. You are simply adding the tongue to the previous exercise. Use the tip of the tongue lightly. The aim is to use the tongue as lightly and effectively as possible. Try to keep the lips still – you can check in a mirror to see if there is any movement,.

An important point: articulation involves the use of muscles, perhaps little used muscles! It will be more effective and you will get results in a shorter time if this is practised little and often. An effective way would be to interrupt other practice routines, perhaps every 10 minutes, with short bursts or articulation practice. Little and often really will get results in the shortest time.

* There is a section on this technique in Practice Book 6 – Advanced Practice.
** Same as a water supply: the on and off action is more immediate when the tap is closest to the end of the hose.

Fast Single Tonguing

Practise Exercise 1 observing the rhythm carefully; the ratio between the first two notes is 3:1 not 2:1. Don't allow it to sound too relaxed. It is a difficult rhythm to single tongue, so as before, little and often is the rule.

To sum up:

- Don't even think about using double tonguing at this stage. It is cheating.
- Practise Exercises 1–20 both loudly and softly.
- Strive to get a clear tlone, especially when ascending to the second octave – that middle E problem!
- Little and often will get the best results especially if you slightly increase the speed every day.
- Play this exercise in other keys. The full exercise is printed in Complete Daily Exercises.

After a few days, change the rhythm to double dotted notes:

The ratio between the first two notes is now 7:1, which is not easy but good articulation practice. Be sure the second note is heard. Play it in the other keys too. As you play faster, in order to coordinate the fingers and tongue, practise in this way:

An *articulation* exercise is a *tone* exercise.

This is more difficult, but to help keep the rhythm accurate, accent with your breath and tap your foot on the first note of every beat.

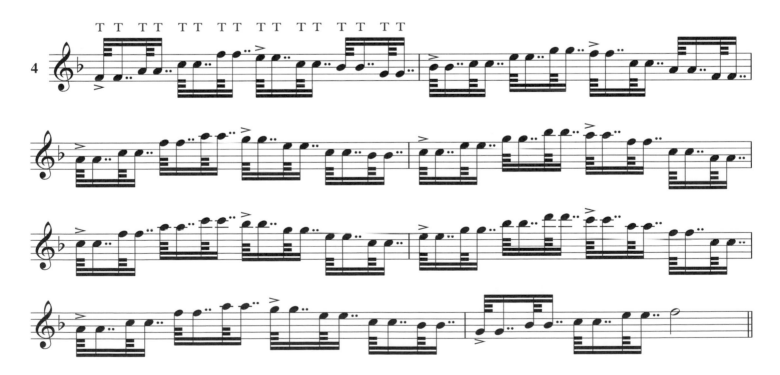

To increase the speed of single tonguing further, practise a few keys in this way. Notice the metronome mark:

As your single tonguing becomes more assured, the abdominal muscles will take a smaller part in forming the note but will continue to give some bounce and will also support the tone.

The tongue has to work harder now. Keep the tongue movement forward and with a light action. Be sure not to move your lips.

As the tongue becomes stronger, so the muscles can maintain single tonguing for longer periods.

Throughout the exercises, and those which follow, practise with a good tone. *An articulation exercise is also a tone exercise.*

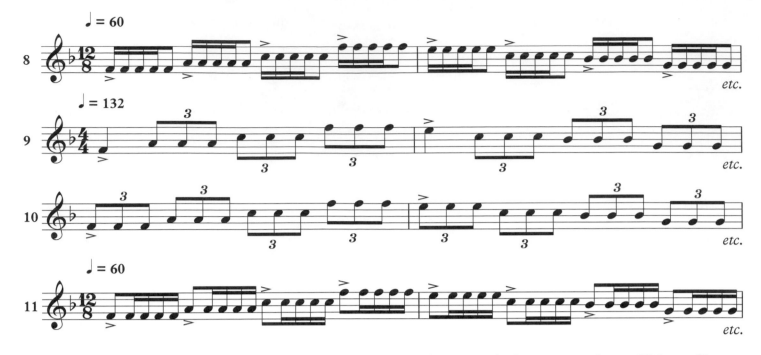

There is often a difficulty when the notes are so arranged that the tongue is thrown out of gear. This conflict between brain and tongue must be addressed. Books of Studies, such as those of Marcel Moyse, often contain exercises to overcome this problem.

Here are some more variations which will help with this issue:

Now to increase the speed further:

If you have had difficulty in gaining some velocity in previous exercises, try these variations. They are, in any case, good practice material.

Do not shorten the last note of a slur.

Whilst slurring, the tongue is resting, and by gradually removing the slurs the tongue works a little harder and becomes stronger.

Remember: before practising this next section, a good control of single tonguing will save time and will help the other forms of articulation. Plenty of time spent on the previous exercises will be most rewarding. You must be the master of your tongue, not its servant!

PROBLEMS BOX

- Exercises 1 & 2 on pages 11–12 are difficult? Spend more time on them. Many find this difficult as you are training a muscle, the tongue, to move quickly, lightly and accurately. It takes time.
- Your tongue is in advance of your fingers? Probably coordination problems. Practise technical exercises in *Practice Book Two – Technique*, to help your fingers move faster and more accurately.
- The tone is unclear when tonguing? For some people it is more difficult than for others to make the tongue move quickly, neatly and yet gently. Sometimes the cause is that the base of the tongue moves as well; in fact the whole muscle moves when articulating. This causes turbulence in the mouth as the air is passing through. In time, and with thoughtful practice, the articulation movement will gradually transfer only to the tip of the tongue. This will make a cleaner attack to each note without sounding explosive.
- Remember that *'an articulation exercise is a tone exercise'*.

ARTICULATION Double Tonguing

Don't start on this section too soon. It's much better to have a good mastery of single tonguing before attempting this technique. As recommended previously, the first part of a double tongued note should be forward against the teeth, illustrated by the letter 'T' and not 'D'. This is because the 'T' sound moves the tongue in a more forward position, and the reflex 'K' will also move forward. In time and with practice, this will result in a clearer articulation.

The reflex action 'K' is usually weaker that the 'T' and that should be corrected. There are exercises below which will help you. Reverse the tongue movement so as to place the accent on the 'back stroke', the 'K'. Work at Exercise 1 with K-T-K-T-K. Do this for all the exercises. Good work on double tonguing can be achieved without the flute because the tongue needs practice in this movement for which the flute isn't necessary. Work at double tonguing both with and without the flute, such as when walking; it will speed up the learning process.

Double tonguing should be practised in small portions at a fast speed: this will get the quickest results. Keep in mind that *'an articulation exercise is a tone exercise'*.

Below is the basic scale exercise shown in the various forms displayed on the next pages from 1–21.

Take a look at this exercise and then begin with Exercise 1 on the next page.

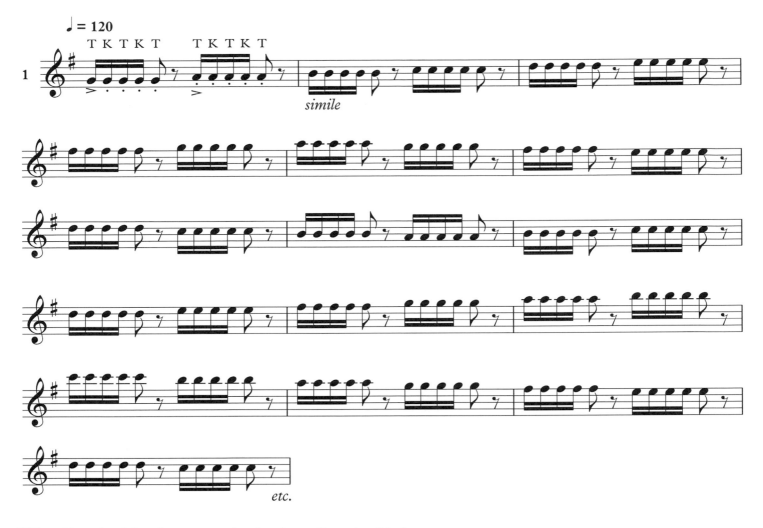

When Exercise 1 has become easier, begin on Exercise 2 below:

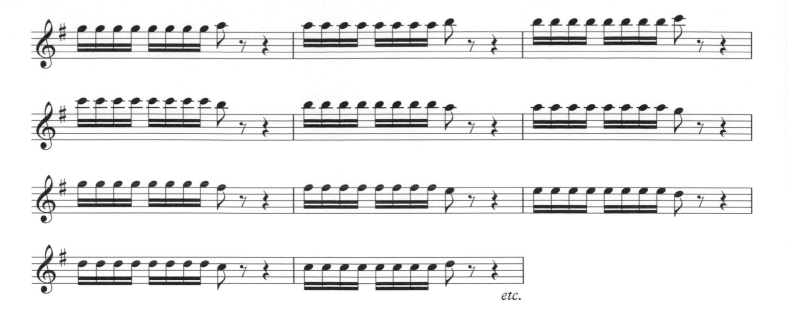

etc.

Train your tongue to be rhythmic, precise and neat.

simile

etc.

simile

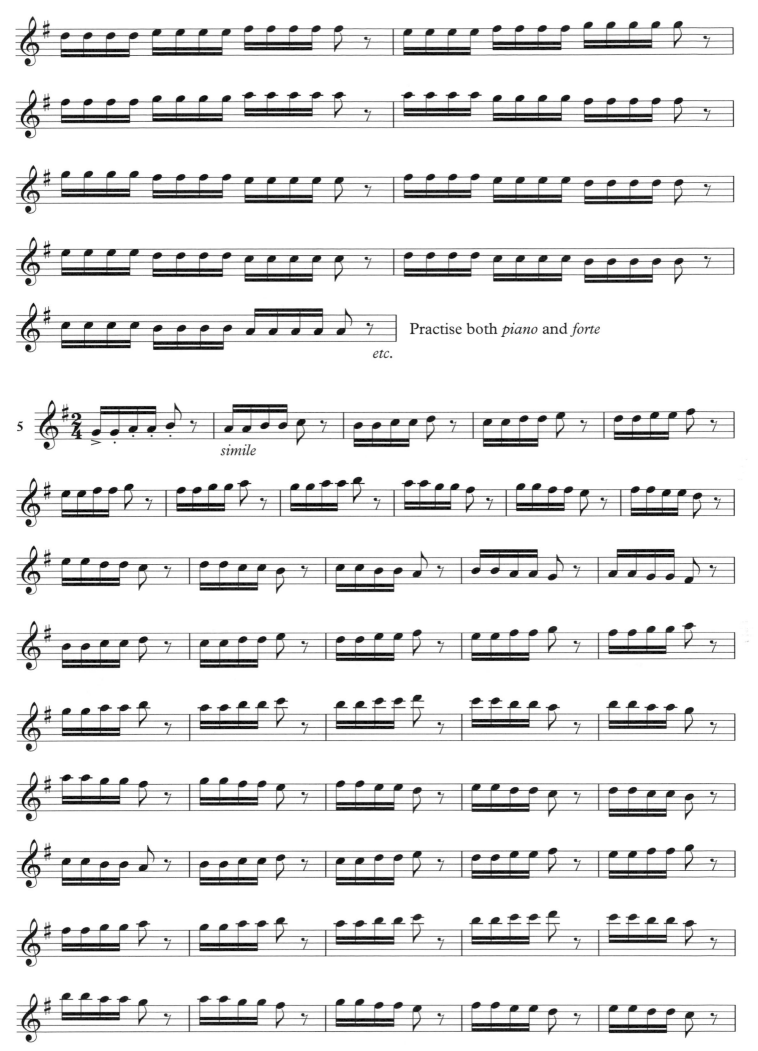

Practise both *piano* and *forte*

etc.

simile

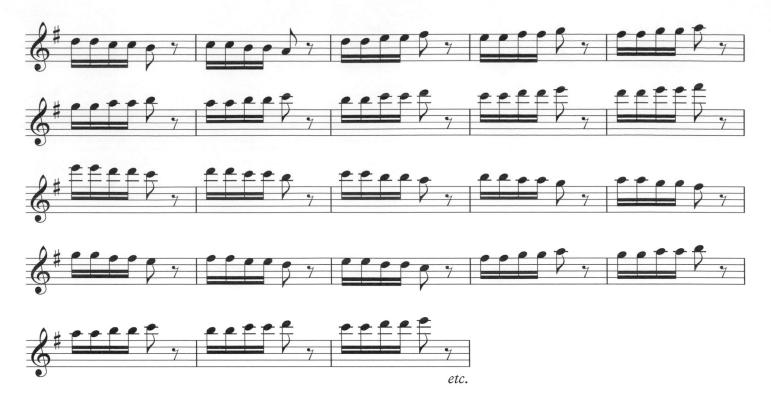

Don't practise double tonguing slowly; it should become a reflex action after the initial 'T' sound is made. As the speed increases, the exercises become more a practice of coordinating the fingers with the tongue, especially in Exercise 8 on the next page.

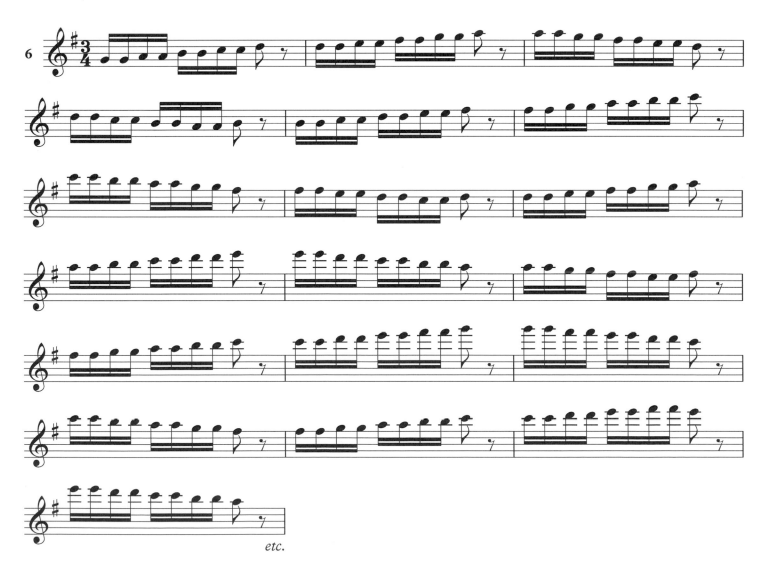

etc.

etc.

Practise the whole study, not just one line. Try other keys too; the full exercise can be found in *Practice Book 5 – Breathing & Scales* or in *The Complete Daily Exercises*.

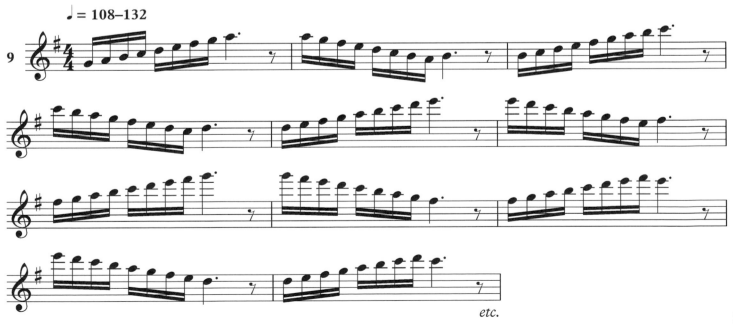

etc.

As in the single tonguing exercises earlier, slurs can be added occasionally to give the tongue a rest. As your tongue becomes more rapid, so some slurs can be omitted.

Remember not to shorten the second note of a slur; it gives a clipped and abrupt sense to the music. Practise these exercises both loudly and softly.

In the next exercise, not only is your tongue exercised but your brain too. The misplacing of the strong downbeat is confusing, but is excellent practice.

Push your tongue to move as fast as possible. Remember to articulate with a good tone.

Play these exercises in other keys. If in difficulty, they are written out fully in *Practice Book 5 – Breathing & Scales* or in *The Complete Daily Exercises*.

PROBLEMS BOX

- You can't get your tongue to move fast enough? Practise – without the flute – on buses, trains, or even when walking. Don't use the flute as a piece of gymnastic apparatus. Tongue forward in the mouth – near the teeth. As the weeks go by, the base of the tongue – which is creating such an upheaval in the mouth – will move less and less and most of the action will be in the tip of the tongue. This will result in a clearer articulation.
- Your tongue gets tired? That's quite normal. Exercise it every day both with and without the flute. When the tongue gets really tired, have a *legato* exercise on the music stand to practise for a few moments to provide a rest for the muscles – then continue tonguing.
- Your articulation limps with the 'K' weaker than the 'T', like this?

That too is a common problem. Starting off with the back stroke ('K') play the double tonguing exercise all the way through. Also practise saying it, starting with 'K'. Put accents on all 'K's. It will help to get rid of unevenness.

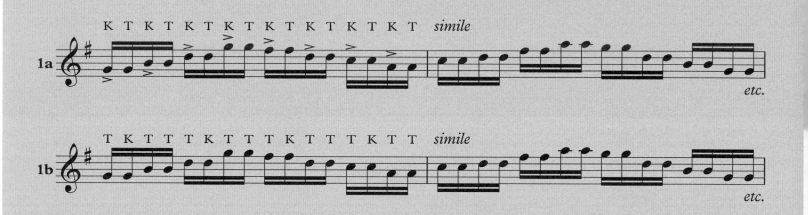

These exercises have no direct musical value, but they are very important if you wish to have complete freedom of articulation both in your muscles and in your mind. And, more importantly, they are most beneficial in securing coordination between the fingers and tongue.

- If after a lot of practice your tone while articulating is not clear or to your liking, try bending the left-hand note C up and down in pitch while articulating. See the Pitch Control section in *Practice Book One – Tone*. Be patient.

ARTICULATION Triple Tonguing

By now you will be familiar with the system of practising articulation. Little and often is the quickest way. To begin, here is a different exercise, though the exercise used for double tonguing is perfectly adequate too. This is the basic Study upon which Exercises 1–13 are built:

(after Reichert)

There are two opinions about the sounds to be used in triple tonguing: some suggest using double tonguing in triple time: 'T-k-t-T-k-t', which is the most common method. Others suggest 'T-k-t-**K**-t-k-**T**-k-t-**K**-t-k'. In fact, both have their uses and you are advised to practise both methods, although the first method more frequently as it will be more useful.

Take a look at these points. They will save you time:

- Practise both kinds of triple tonguing without the flute, such as when walking.
- Tongue forward. In the long term, it will give you the best result and be clearer and neater.
- Remember that *an articulation exercise is a tone exercise.*
- The use of both tongue and breath (air speed) differ in loud and soft playing so remember to practise both.
- Increase the speed regularly. Use a metronome; your memory of yesterday's tempo may not be reliable.
- Practise a little and often.

Don't go on until you feel you could play No. 6 in public!

Practise the exercises all the way through, not just a few bars.

This next one is for a bit of fun:

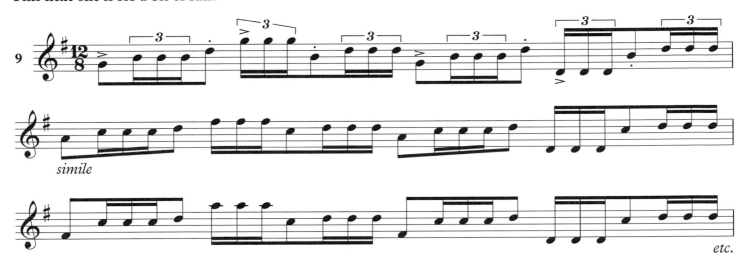

In order to obtain complete freedom of your tongue and your unconscious reflexes, it would be wise to practise the exercises like this:

When you tackle these, you will understand the problem!

The exercises above are only an outline of a method of many, many months of careful practice, and the principle should be applied to all kinds of studies.

Some examples of double and triple tonguing will be found at the end of this book.

ARTICULATION Cracking Notes

E♭ and other notes in the right hand

For both acoustic and constructional reasons, the right hand notes of the second octave are prone to 'cracking' or 'splitting'. The right air speed is essential at the start of the note to make them secure. It is perhaps strange, but worthwhile to practise this effect so as to become familiar with the problem, and then it is easier to overcome it. Most often, the cause of 'cracking' is that the first finger is left on the C♯ key when it should be removed for E♭ and D. Even if the first finger is taken off – but too late, after the E♭ has started to sound – it will still result in 'cracking'.

Play Exercise 1 with the first finger down for E♭. Play it short and loud to hear how unpleasant it is. Then repeat with the first finger removed, the correct fingering. This will help your ear to recognise the problem and to fix it.

Do the same for Exercise 2 but keeping the first finger down for both E♭ and D.

Now move on to Exercise 3 but finger C as you would for the lowest C. Notice how the 'cracking' gets worse.

Do the same for Exercise 4; keep the first finger on for E♭. Play it both slurred and *staccato*. Notice how much worse it sounds when tongued. In fact the 'cracking' takes place usually only at the start of the E♭, so as your technique becomes faster, the E♭ becomes relatively shorter and the 'cracking' takes up a larger proportion of the note! In brief: the faster you play, the worse it sounds.

*The most frequently recurring fault found in young players. Theobald Boehm, who designed our flute, also designed E♭ and D to be played with the first finger raised. *Top* E♭ should, of course, be played with *all* fingers down.

THREE E♭ EXERCISES

These exercises were written especially to practise removing the first finger for E♭ and D *at the start of the note*. When you can play it through without mistakes, both *legato* and *staccato*, you have made good progress.

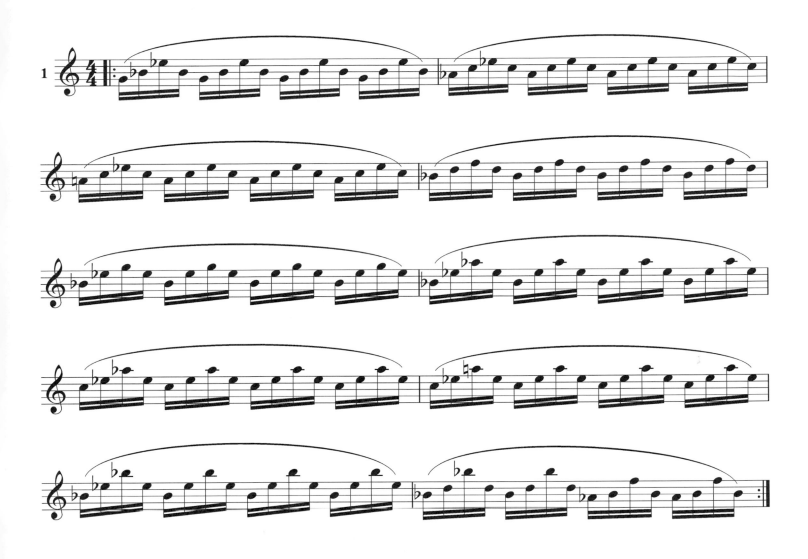

Play the next exercise twice through. If you should play even one bad E♭ – or a D natural with the 1st finger on – then go back and repeat. Continue repeating until faultless. Then try four times through without a mistake. Eight times through and you have done well. *No cheating!*

Besides concentrating on ensuring that the first finger is off for E♭, be sure also to use the D♯ key for all notes except D natural. You will really have to concentrate in this study.

OVERCOMING NERVES IN PERFORMANCE

Everyone seems to suffer – and benefit – from nerves when performing. A performer who claims never to be nervous is a rare person indeed. Moreover, we are all different in how nerves affect us. For some, it means shaking knees, a dry mouth, queasy stomach, fingers shaking, breaking into a sweat, dry tongue, a feeling of panic, etc. Others claim to have quite different emotions and experiences. Yet nervousness can sometimes improve the performance.

In response to instructions from the brain, which are sent when we are under stress, substances are released by the brain. These then transmit signals to glands in various parts of the body to release adrenaline. In other, more primal circumstances, adrenaline would assist you in running faster to escape, or to retaliate when under attack and these actions would in turn burn up the adrenaline. In a musical performer, this adrenaline is simply not being burnt up and it is this unused adrenaline which causes the unpleasant and unhelpful effects mentioned above. There are a number of ways to tackle the problem so as to perform relatively free from the debilitating nervousness which spoils a performance, perhaps even turning it around so as to enhance the performance.

Some teachers recommend deep breathing, lying on your back with knees bent (such as used by the Alexander technique and by actors), sucking boiled sweets or barley sugar, eating a banana and avoiding stimulants such as caffeine.

Another way is to tackle the problem face on: when performing next, while announcing the pieces, stand with your legs apart, hand behind your back if possible and talk to the audience, looking at their faces. This approach is used by actors too. Its purpose is to become aware that the audience are your friends and amiably disposed towards you. Taking every available opportunity to perform is also helpful as your fear of performing will normally diminish as time goes on.

In the past thirty years, a growing number of clinics, self-help courses, therapies and workshops have developed, all claiming to tackle and cure the problem of nerves. If this is the way you wish to go, ask around to find out what kind of course might appeal to you. At national flute conventions, there are workshops which may give a good idea of which approach a particular teacher has. It has even become possible to do this online.

To tackle the problem in a natural way is the best solution but not the only one. In very severe cases, if you are suffering extreme episodes – similar to panic attacks – it would be best to consult your doctor. Doctors may prescribe beta-blockers, a drug widely used by those with heart problems, which can prevent the symptoms of anxiety, and break the 'fear cycle'. Your doctor may also prescribe a course of cognitive behavioural therapy to help you address the cause of your anxiety.

The bottom line is this – after years of study you have reached a high level of performing. The important concert or audition is approaching. To take a chance on playing at a level lower than you are accustomed to may result in not getting the job.

Take action – whichever path you choose.

EXAMPLES: Melodies from the Flute Repertoire

DOUBLE TONGUING

CONCERTO IN D MINOR

C.P.E. BACH

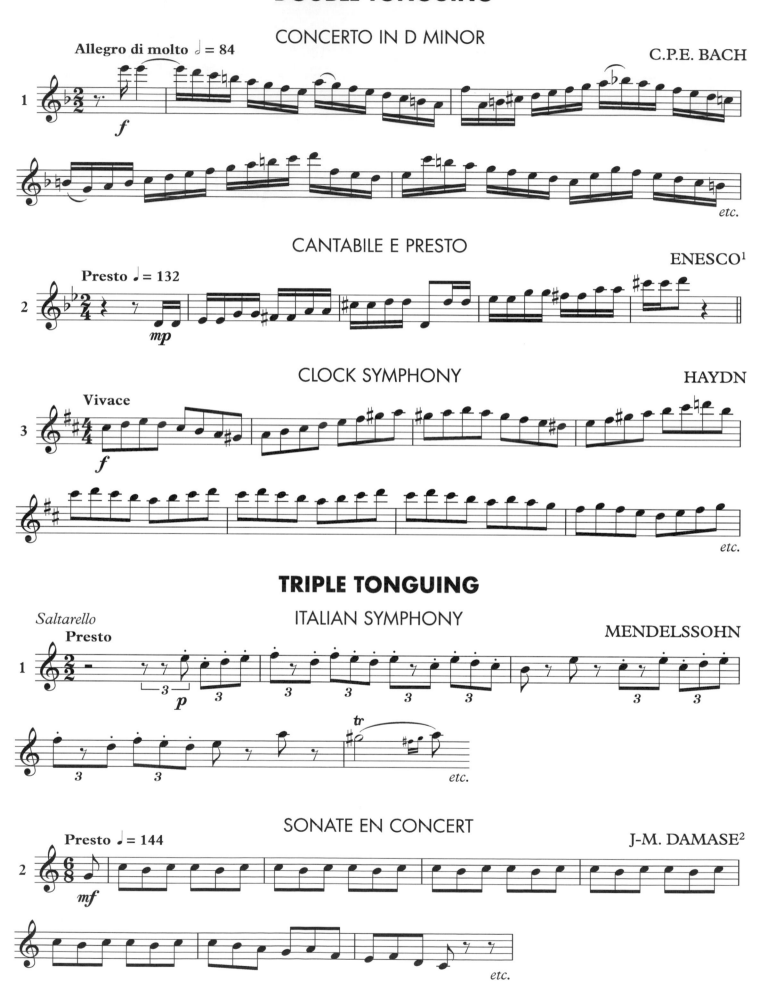

CANTABILE E PRESTO

ENESCO[1]

CLOCK SYMPHONY

HAYDN

TRIPLE TONGUING

ITALIAN SYMPHONY

MENDELSSOHN

SONATE EN CONCERT

J-M. DAMASE[2]

 [1]Reproduced by permission of Enoch et Cie - Paris, U.K. and Commonwealth agents Edwin Ashdown Ltd.
[2]Editions Lemoine, Paris / United Music Publishers Ltd. By permission.